Living In The Light

A Guide To Discovering & Manifesting Your Life Purpose

Written by
Jasmine Clemente

Copyright © 2020 Jasmine Clemente

All rights reserved. No part of this publication may be reproduced, distributed, or transmitted in any form or by any means, including photocopying, recording, or other electronic or mechanical methods, without the prior written permission of the publisher, except in the case of brief quotations embodied in critical reviews and certain other noncommercial uses permitted by copyright law.

Photography by Manny Cabo

Book Design by : HMDpublishing

ACKNOWLEDGMENTS

To my Father and Mother,

You were the perfect match to create me in order to fulfill my mission and share the kind of knowledge and wisdom in the way that I do.

All of the black and white classic movies that my father had me watch broadened my horizons, allowing me to see that no matter how old or new something is, there is no time and space that can diminish the value of a great message, or the quality of a great moment.

All of the Ancient Alien TV shows that my mother had me watch kept reminding me of my original origin which is beyond this world. As my mother, she made me remember that we are much, much more than just this physical body living in this lifetime. Hence, our favorite talk show host, Oprah, solidified this.

To some of the coolest friends on Earth,

August Tarantino –

Thank you for sitting across from me at The Ananda Ashram Yoga Retreat where we chatted it up, only to find out you'd become one of my writing mentors and the one to guide me with self-publishing!

Edwin Vazquez –

Thank you for always sharing your spiritual outlook as a friend for true healing. I used one of the biblical quotes you shared with me in Chapter Two.

Susan Shapiro –

Thank you for taking me under your wing as one of your writing students! Despite the many years that have passed, you gave me the confidence to publish a book because of all the advice you gave, the resources you generously shared, and the classes you taught.

Cynthia Sepulveda –

Thank you for being the kind of friend who supported my many transitions in life. We've shared many secrets, and you've gotten me through some of the toughest times which allowed me to continue living in my light.

Roai Saiag –

Toda Raba! Thank you for teaching me how to speak one of the most ancient languages of the world, which I hold dear to my heart: Hebrew. You are a part of my soul tribe.

John Hawkins –

Thank you for giving me the courage to travel alone. Because of your advice, I had one of the most magical vacations in my life when I visited Sedona, Arizona right before the pandemic hit.

To all of my family & friends whom I didn't mention (and even my furry little pets) -

Every person whom I've had the honor to share time with hold gifts that remind me of the seasons: divine, unique, and with deep purpose. Although things change, we'll always circle back home.

CONTENTS

ACKNOWLEDGMENTS

PART 1
Rebirth 13

CHAPTER ONE:
INNOCENCE & INTUITION 15

CHAPTER TWO:
FRUITFULNESS 35

CHAPTER THREE:
FORGIVENESS 49

PART 2
Metamorphosis 71

CHAPTER FOUR:
CLARITY 73

CHAPTER FIVE:
LEAP OF FAITH 85

CHAPTER SIX:
LOVE 99

CHAPTER SEVEN:
PASSING THE TORCH 111

BIO

Living In The Light

Forget what you think you know, because none of us know everything except for a few subtle hints provided by the whispers and memories of our soul.

HOW TO USE THIS MANUAL

Before reading this book, I recommend taking a shower first to wash off the old energetic debris you absorbed from the day. As the water cleanses your body, tell yourself that you release all that is no longer serving you, and that you desire to clean your mind and heart from all negative thoughts. After stepping out of the shower and drying yourself off, you should feel lighter and fresher. That's when you should light a white candle and do a fifteen-minute meditation in a quiet place where you won't be disturbed. It'll clear your mind so that you can focus on the literature you're about to intake. Remember, this manual is designed for you to live in the light which means to remember your divinity. This isn't a guideline for you to just attract what you think want or think you need. It's for you to attract what is healthy, abundant and true whether you have been awakened to your higher self or not. The way to live your true purpose is by first remembering your divinity because if your spiritual foundation isn't understood, respected and nurtured, then what you may think your purpose is may just be an illusion that will eventually backfire even if you manifest it.

> **"Although we live in the world, we are not of the world."**

– Biblical Corinthians 10:3

Discovering and manifesting are two different things. To discover something, means that it already exists but has yet to be found. However, to manifest something means it does not yet exist, but can be created. Thus, when discovering and manifesting your life purpose, you must first realize that your purpose is already within waiting for you to discover it, and once you do, then you can manifest more of it just like a sorcerer.

TWO PART BOOK

- **PART ONE IS CALLED REBIRTH** which consists of three chapters: Innocence, Fruitfulness, and Forgiveness. This is because you must destroy your old identity in order to rebuild a new one. But who says your old identity should be destroyed? Maybe it doesn't. You'll know as you read through these pages if it should.

- **PART TWO IS CALLED METAMORPHOSIS** which consists of four chapters: Clarity, Leap of Faith, Love, and Pass The Torch. Once you understand the first part of this book, you'll have a powerful burst of energy to do what you love to do, and this is when transformation happens.

PART 1

Rebirth

The action of reappearing or starting to flourish or increase after a decline; revival.

CHAPTER One:
INNOCENCE & INTUITION

There's something about that feeling you get when walking along the beach shore; the way the sea salt water gently crashes over your feet, washing away the debris of yesterday from the places you've been.

Your footprints gently fade into the wet sand until they disappear, freeing you from an expired memory. And as you face yourself to the sun, feeling the warm breeze blow your cares away, you thank God for moments like this; that you can cleanse your aura and start brand new.

But every day doesn't feel so heavenly. And this is why you reflect on how to break certain patterns and avoid drama at all costs in hopes that you'll never have to repeat a bad cycle again. But as they say, "When one door closes, another one opens." And so, cycles are a part of life. We just want to make sure that as certain situations end, we are cycling upwards instead of downwards towards better tomorrows.

INNOCENCE & INTUITION

In this book I'll share some personal experiences that kept me in the shadows. Sometimes I'd know that something was "off," but other times I was just unaware. Either way, I currently have no desire to live in the past now that I've arrived at a healthy and prosperous present day future. But it took disappointment after disappointment before realizing that I had to let my old identity die before I could let my real identity live; that is, my true spiritual nature.

Talking about spirits. I remember one profound moment where a spirit crossed over, leaving his earthly existence. I got the news after sleeping from anesthesia in the surgery room. The vibration of my cellphone buzzed with a message from my ex-fiancés best friend.

Ironically, while doctors had been removing a polyp from my cervix which was blocking my possibilities of getting pregnant, my ex fiancé was on life support with 24 hours left to live in a different hospital.

Grief..

Never had I understood the meaning of that word until experiencing it the way I did.

Eventually I left the hospital to come home, but instead of celebrating my possibility of having a baby before 40, all I could do was cry, uncontrollably, on my kitchen floor.

The cause of his death is still a little unclear as it was a mixture of many things: Lung Cancer, Kidney Failure and Drug Addiction.

But I begin this chapter with him because of the unseen link between open and closed doors. On a day when I had thought I'd be celebrating the fact that I could finally conceive a child, my ex had taken his last breath as they pulled the plug. Talk about polarities.

I suddenly remembered when we were strangers and how innocent our relationship used to be. I knew nothing of his inner demons and he knew nothing of mine. In the beginning, all we knew was how good we made each other feel, and for a while, we lit each other up.

It's like we brought the inner child out of each other, which leads me to the following point.

We're not kids anymore but yet, in some ways we are. Because we're always growing, developing, and questioning things, we

INNOCENCE & INTUITION

are eternal students that look like we've reached adulthood when approaching a certain age, but beneath the surface we're like babies compared to the grandiosity of what the universe still has to teach us. Think about it. Regardless of whether you're in your twenties, thirties, forties, fifties or sixties, don't you learn something new every day? And unlearn things too?

In that regard, I've found a happy medium between taking life too seriously and making time for playful, childlike wonder because you really don't know when this will all be over.

You can be a responsible adult whose able to stand on your own two feet and still make time for adventure. Who says life has to be boring just because the bills gotta get paid?

It goes deeper than that.

Who says you have to remain in a loveless marriage? Accept defeat from illness? Stay addicted to toxicity? Or feel helpless in an abusive situation?

For many years, my ex had a victimhood mentality. Due to his toxic lifestyle of abusing drugs, alcohol, cigarettes and cigars, he had created disease within the body.

When I viewed his open casket, I just kept wishing that he would've fought the good fight to overcome his self-destructive ways. Unfortunately, for him, it was too late. But who knows if he'll reincarnate to get it right the second or hundredth time around, such as the mysteries of life?

Sometimes Adults lose their sense of leadership because we don't know how to break free from a situation that pins us down. But whether you're stuck in a rut or taking time to soul search, I want you to know that deep inside lies a spiritual power that can change your situation almost overnight, miraculously.

Yea right? You're thinking... Overnight? Yes, because DECISIONS ARE THAT POWERFUL.

Before my ex had died, I saw the train wreck coming long before we'd broken up which is why I left him. It was one of the hardest decisions I ever made because I felt like I was abandoning the love of my life. But he refused rehab in a quick fit of rage, strangling my neck one day in his NJ apartment, so for me, it came down to an ultimatum. Either I was going to stay with someone dragging me down, or I was going to rise up and save myself.

INNOCENCE & INTUITION

It had been late night, early morning. Around 3:00 a.m. on a Sunday night. I was at a nightclub, performing one of my records for a crowd of vibrant house heads. When I finished singing, I put my microphone down and saw my ex inside the DJ booth sniffing a line of coke while arguing with a friend. Since he was already distracted, I took the opportunity to sneak off by heading towards the bathroom.

I figured that by pretending to use the bathroom, no one would see me leave. Getting lost in the crowd, I bumped into the shoulders of drunk women wobbling in stilettos, others spinning in circles to the music, and men yelling for more rounds at the bar. Eventually, I reached the club's exit sign without ever having to say goodbye – to anyone.

As soon as I pushed the door open and hit the cold, crisp, wind, I gasped for air. I had escaped him, feeling an uncanny sense of freedom. It was like I had released myself from a monstrous grip, but I had to first scream before I could shout.

That night changed my life forever. I still loved him. I still wanted to save him. I still wanted to change him. I still wanted him to see what I saw: that life can either be heaven or hell. But he had chosen his hell while I, with broken wings, had chosen to flee.

In the morning, I awoke in my own bedroom and washed my hands clean of him. I told myself to never go back. And for one whole year, I ignored him, while reflecting back to myself.

You see, I was an underground Recording House Artist performing in various nightclubs throughout NYC. My ex fiancé wasn't the only person to indulge in coke, alcohol, weed, ecstasy, molly pills, you name it. The club scene reeked of near death experiences. But I loved the music, the congas, the jumping up and down in euphoric bliss. I just didn't like the evil spirits that lingered amidst toxic substances.

As I removed myself from the club scene, I began to question why I started this musical journey in the first place? It wasn't about "regrets," but it was more about "intention." Who were my earlier role models? What had influenced me? Did it still serve my highest good? Did I just need a break? Did I need change? This is where "choice" comes in. I decided to peel away all the layers of myself until I got to the source. In starting over, I became like a child.

INNOCENCE & INTUITION

When realizing that the power of choice can change your situation overnight, you have to understand why you made that choice, so that you don't repeat the same mistake. In fact, it's not only about making new choices, it's about making the best choices.

The power of choice will change your perspective which will then CHANGE HOW YOU FEEL...

which will then CHANGE WHAT YOU ATTRACT...

which will then CHANGE YOUR LIFE.

But first, you must be like a child.

Let's go deeper for a minute.

To be like a child means to remember another time and another place. That is, another world.

Before you were born, you were very much alive inside of your mother's womb, breathing, sleeping, and receiving nutrients even though you knew nothing about the outside world. But think about it: If you once traveled outside of her womb to be born, then where were you *before* her womb?

I'll repeat that.

If you once traveled outside of her womb to be born, then where were you *before* her womb?

Now, to remember where you were before you entered her womb, you might have to remember who or what you used to be.

Since Science hasn't proven where souls come from, let's call our souls "energy" for arguments sake.

"Energy" is what turns on a light bulb, makes the water flow, gives breath to animals, and makes trees grow. And since we are energy, there is no beginning and there is no end, but there are points in which we change form, such as when a caterpillar turns into a butterfly, or when someone dies and moves into another dimension. For better or for worse, even the very nature of things change given enough time.

They say that babies and children are innocent because they don't know the dark side of adults. For example, children are taught racism, bullying, greed, political history, and they're even taught abuse if they've witnessed it growing up. Thus, since babies are born innocent before learning any of this, that means that when we were babies, we were once innocent too! (Including my ex-fiance before growing up to adapt a toxic lifestyle, like so many others. Yes, even my ex-fiance was once a completely... innocent... baby.)

What opinions, habits, and lifestyle choices do you have that caused havoc in your life? Can you identify them? Perhaps there are things you were taught to believe were right, but turned out to be wrong?

Did you grow up with abusive parents? Conceited parents? Alcoholics? Or was your family pretty normal but highly judgmental, unforgiving, and rigid? Did you grow up in a racist town? Did you grow up poor or rich? Was money a dominant factor in your childhood?

In order to live in the light, we have to know what is not of the light so we don't support an illusion. Therefore, before discovering and manifesting your life purpose, let's first make sure that what you desire is wholesome, peaceful, vibrant, healthy, fair and true. Because what you learned may or may not have been.

I'm living proof that I didn't have a perfect childhood, nor did I attract a perfect future because of it. I'm not blaming my parents, or society or even God. I just recognize that my misfortunes weren't an accident. There were behaviors I learned by observing my surroundings growing up; things I learned to accept as truth and habits that I grew into. Hence, the only way to really unlearn some of the unhealthiness that was unconsciously passed down to me, was to trust my own inner GPS.

We all have an intuition; some feel it more than others. And this intuition we feel is not something outside of ourselves; it is within.

Intuition is connected to our soul; our energy life force. It is connected to the part of us from when we lived inside of our mother's womb, and even before we entered her womb.

Our intuition gives us direction like a map that points us left or right, to continue going straight ahead or warning us to turn back. So when discovering and manifesting our life's purpose, it's very important that we trust this inner voice above all other voices.

Our intuition was there when we were children, but because we were being taught which language to speak, which school to attend, what clothes to wear, what foods to eat, what careers to choose, what kinds of people to socialize with, what kinds of music to listen to and so forth, the whispers of our intuition drowned out from all the other voices we were bombarded with. How could you hear or feel your own intuition if every day you were being told what to do because you were just a child? Although our parents may have had good intentions to prepare us for the future, our intuition most likely weakened. Thus, we were left with the power of our mind because that is the muscle we exercised most. However, the challenge with that is that our minds could've been brainwashed. So I ask you, at what age do you think you stopped hearing or feeling YOUR INTUITION?

Let's go back to what it means to manifest our life purpose. Knowing how our brains have absorbed so much information throughout the years that it most likely weakened our intuition, how do we know when we're manifesting our true life purpose or when we're manifesting what we *think* we want but actually isn't good for us?

To be like a child means to empty our minds and start fresh.

Let... It... All... Go...

Pretend that your life is a blank page and that you don't know your family, your friends, your coworkers, your classmates, your neighbors, or the celebrities you watch on TV. Pretend, for just a little while, that you are like Keanu Reeves in the Matrix, and your entire world as you know it just disappeared and you are floating within a clear, blank, white room without any furniture or walls.

Now that you hold an empty white image in your mind, let's begin to fill it with some things...

If you were born a different gender, a different race, in a different country and in a different time, do you think you'd still like the things that you like right now or want the things you want? (Like, would I have still wanted to be a Recording House Music Singer if I was raised in Switzerland to NASA Scientists for parents?) Just imagine how much of what you think is good for you has been influenced by your surroundings, your culture, and your upbringing?

If you can destroy your identity as you know it today, then imagine how you can rebuild and recreate it tomorrow? In fact, maybe you're like a beautiful sandcastle by the shore that can never die even after the ocean tide washes over it because sand doesn't disappear. And what if (in that same breath) you don't know yet that you being a particle of sand can actually turn into a pearl?

To discover and manifest your life purpose, try these three things:

- Be like a child and pretend you are in that empty space that I just mentioned and remove all prejudices, judgements, and any unloving traits that are popular in the world but do not serve your highest good. (Like drugs and alcohol for example. Just because everyone else does it, doesn't mean you should too.)

- Remember that you are more than just your body. You are an energy that traveled into this world (like when you rested within your mother's womb) and you will continue to travel after your physical life ends here.

- Exercise your intuition by trusting your inner knowing above all other voices and outside opinions. Your intuition is your divine GPS guiding you to fulfill your life's purpose; not to go against it.

- Because your purpose is connected to the light, do not engage in dark activities (such as backstabbing people to make it to the top even if "becoming successful at all costs" is accepted by popular culture.) They don't have long lasting sustainability because success achieved through negative actions will reap negative consequences. **Note: You wouldn't want to be the man who gained the world but lost his soul in it, would you?**

- Take your time and be patient when discovering your purpose. Time is an illusion on earth that will make you race to get what you think you want, but you'll end up missing out on what matters most because you never took the time to smell the roses.

To live in the light, you must be the light. But how can you be the light if you're disconnected from it? There's truth to our ancient biblical scriptures such as, "Although we live in the world, we are not of the world."

To not be of the world, sounds like we are here renting space because we are not of the same fabric as planet earth. Perhaps our souls, (which is energy) is of a different source beyond this planet but we've been brainwashed to forget our true spiritual nature. We are here living in the world temporarily as if we're inside a classroom that has a finishing point once the lesson's over. And yet there are those who actually believe hell is on Earth. I would imagine that soldiers who fought and killed in wars would perceive it this way, or anyone dealing with inner conflict. But whatever this place means to you, none of us are meant to stay here forever.

Within this temporary journey, what do you think your reason is for being here? Is it to be a mother; the best mother one can be? Is it to be a Doctor; saving lives from tragic accidents and chronic illnesses? Is it to be a filmmaker; creating works of art that will relay messages across the big screen to the masses? Or is it to be a Singer; writing songs that will inspire generations? Whatever you feel your purpose is, you'll know it's right when you feel peace within your soul. Anything that will advance the consciousness of human kind is light expressing itself through the vessel of a clear and willing participant.

Are you that willing participant? Are you an open vessel willing to receive divine inspiration and to execute them when your intuition propels you to move forward?

I'm not suggesting to block people's opinions out completely, but if they offer you their two sense on what career you should pursue, and who you should love and how you should live your life, make sure that their opinions match your intuitive hunch before taking their advice. Remember, you've been influenced by people since the day you were born. When will you start trusting your own intuition which is of a supernatural divinity - and always of the light?

If you don't know how to trust your intuition because it's been weakened, carve out some time to be alone in silence and meditate. The more you recharge your batteries by spending "alone" time, the more you can hear the whispers of your spirit. It is there where innocence dwells because your intuition only wants to serve love and make everything better, sort of like a child who sees nothing wrong playing in the sandbox with different shades of kids because they haven't yet been exposed to racism. Hence, one of the ways to discover your life's purpose is to start all over again and be like a child. But this time, you can censor how much information you're choosing to receive so you're not bombarded by other people's opinions (except your own spiritual GPS).

CHAPTER Two:

FRUITFULNESS

A Christian friend once told me, "A tree is recognized by its fruit." And furthermore, "No good tree bears bad fruit. And no bad tree bears good fruit." (Luke 6:44)

This sounds to me that the results in our lives started from a root cause. Things don't magically happen without any reason behind them or some action that was taken before hand. In other words, if we neglect to water, feed, and nurture a seed, then we can't expect to save it after it's already grown into full maturity. Thus, there is a time for everything, and time surely does pass.

This brings me back to children. It is so crucial that we teach children to live in the light rather than bombard them with judgmental, discriminative, greedy, and insensitive ways in order to make it in a so-called "doggy dog world." But let's say it's too late for that. We're already adults reading this and our childhood is long gone. And since most of us didn't have a perfect childhood, it wouldn't be smart to start blaming our elders however, it would be wise to start understanding.

So now we're here with a certain personality type and lifestyle that we've adopted, and whether or not we believe it has served us or not, let's examine the fruits.

- Are you in a loving, healthy and thriving relationship with your companion or even with yourself? Or are you in an unhealthy relationship?

- Do you love your job and find yourself wanting to grow with the company? Or do you work there for one reason only – to pay the bills? Do you own your own company and want to continue growing it? Or are you there simply because you don't want to look like a failure if you close it down?

- Do you love your body, your face, your style, and your overall appearance? Or do you wish you looked like someone else? Confidence is the most attractive feature on a person, but are you insecure?

- Do you have the financial support and freedom to plan trips, eat healthy, build your dreams and express yourself to your fullest potential? Or do you feel poor and have to depend on others?

Whatever your life looks like at this time, these are the fruits from the seeds that were planted in the past. The question now is: what seeds will you plant this time around now that you've emptied out your mind from all of your childhood brainwashing? Because now is the time to take responsibility in planting fresh, new seeds so that you can manifest your true life purpose.

I'll give you an example...

Eventually I had to admit that I had a few bad fruits in my life and that wasn't good enough for me. I was ready to revamp my entire garden; meaning clean up my entire life. It started with me healing my finances, healing my physical health, and healing my personal relationships – which ironically meant me cutting the chord with certain people.

It wasn't enough to be out of an abusive relationship with an ex who had died. I had to truly reevaluate all of my relationships, including the biggest one of all: Myself.

I decided to travel.

It was the Summer of 2019. I could've went anywhere in the world and did anything with whomever. But instead I followed the light within like a good little spiritual hermit, taking a window seat on the Coach Bus as I, alone, headed upstate NY to the woodsy bear town of Monroe, and checked into the Yoga Retreat: Ananda Ashram.

It was far from a luxurious vacation. In fact, an old, rundown cab picked me up at the main bus station and drove me down the dusty road to the Ashram which was, thankfully, surrounded by rich green grass and complete utter silence. Slamming the heavy cab door behind me with a broken knob was the least of my concerns.

To breathe fresh air was just what my soul needed.

When looking at how the fruits in my life would multiply, was I going to continue growing weeds and fungus, or a luscious garden that attracted bees and butterflies? This was a metaphor for the kinds of men I'd date, friends I'd have, work I'd create, home I'd live in, and legacy I'd leave behind. Therefore, taking a vacation by myself seemed like the perfect antidote for self-reflection to ensure that going forward, I would make healthier choices for myself.

On my first day at Ananda Ashram, I had decided to get off social media by leaving my cell phone charged inside of my cabin to venture off into the woods undisturbed. It was a little tempting not to snap photos of nature's majestic views, but this was about "me," and I wanted to enjoy my solitude.

Tall, evergreen trees covered every piece of land I walked through, home to cute squirrels that ran in between them, stopping only to nibble on large acorns and walnuts. The air was fresh, unpolluted, and the Summer warmth felt good on my skin; perfect for a free spirited woman wearing a loose fitting Bob Marley T-shirt, tight yoga spandex, and sneakers.

Aimlessly wandering, I came across their famous lake house featuring a wooden kayaking boat, their 3 to 12 foot diving pool, their yoga studio offering daily classes, and their all-you-can-eat Vegan buffet dining hall. But what drew my attention most, were the silent meditation rooms hidden behind closed doors inside of several cabin homes, each one of them complete with alters amidst an array of fresh flowers, sweet smelling incense, and candles to illuminate statues of Indian Deities and Goddesses. Once inside, all foot-ware had to be removed, and silence was golden.

It was in these quiet moments where I would close my eyes, reminisce about anything – absolutely anything – and ask spirit for peaceful closure, guidance, and love.

Before my trip was over, I met a few kindred spirits along my trails. It's like that saying, "You're never really alone." Well, coincidences let you know that the universe is definitely watching you.

Not only was it in the thick of Summer, but it was in the month of August to be exact. And out of all the incredible people I met, there was one who struck out the most; the one I met on my last day at Ananda Ashram before returning home to the city.

His name was August. Yep, that's right. In the month of August, I met a man named August who sat across from me at the Vegan Dining Hall, eating oatmeal and apples, and snacking on some Yogurt.

We made friendly small talk, and while I thought it was quite the coincidence that his name matched the month we were in, I saw it as an even bigger sign that he was a published Author who offered intuitive writing courses and workshops. I was a writer too! Correction... I am a writer. And with that, it made sense that the universe had placed him before me because part of my intention was to meet healthy people (in mind, body and spirit) who I resonated with as I moved forward in my new chapter in life.

After talking a bit, we walked around the lake and shared our interests in yoga, world travels, and of course, writing. He had a lot of valuable insight to offer, and we exchanged information to stay in touch after the trip was over. If anyone thinks that the universe doesn't respond to your wishes and desires, my testimony of meeting a man named August in the month of August who helped me craft my first self-published book should be proof that magic does exist!

Keep reading to see what you'd like to manifest and bring forth into your existence. If it's meant for you and it's wholesome, it'll be fruitful and multiply. If it's not, you can still manifest it, but eventually it'll die off because it won't have lasting power, so make sure it's from the light.

Do you want to manifest a wonderful romantic relationship? A passionate career you feel proud of? A beautiful house? World travel?

Of course the more specific you are, the better. But remember, you also need to first discover what your natural gifts are before you can manifest what you want. Because what you want might not be the best thing for you, and if you try manifesting it, you can find yourself struggling instead of flowing with it.

When discovering your purpose, what do you do easily?

Be careful here because you shouldn't be general. Be specific. For example, if you like to talk a lot, that doesn't necessarily mean you should be a motivational speaker. It might mean that you would make a great radio host (if you're into music or sports, depending on what the radio show is about.) Or let's say you love fashion. That doesn't necessarily mean that you should design your own clothing line. It might mean that you should start your own fashion magazine (if you're also into writing and photography). Is this making sense?

Everything isn't for everybody. And this is what makes us all unique. Everyone isn't going to fall in love with the same kind of person or want the same type of relationship. And everyone isn't going to want the same type of career, want to work for the same company, or even want to live in the same city. So since everyone is different, there's never a reason to compare your life to others or think that what you want isn't valid. You have something that no one else has because of the way you do it. And when you discover what that is, then you'll be able to manifest that which blossoms naturally and will bear good fruit because it's so easy for you to do. What your true purpose in life is should come as easily as breathing. Why try to manifest something that shrinks you or that you'll struggle with?

Seeds are meant to grow. We can't always determine how tall a tree will grow or how many fruits it will bear. But we know it will multiply. This is the law of life. When something is charged with positive energy, it will increase.

Have you payed attention to the things that increase in your life and to the things that decrease? When something dies, it's because its time has passed and there's no room for it anymore. What things are you holding onto that may be preventing you from being fruitful? What things are blocking you from moving forward?

It could be an old dream that has come to pass. I know mainstream media says to "Never Give Up." But that's like a smoker never quitting cigarette's because his pride has tricked him into believing that quitting is for suckers. Have you ever considered that some dreams may not have been in your best interest even though you truly believed they were? Sometimes giving up an old dream creates space for a new dream that will serve you better today. But living in the past will not bring you towards your future any faster. It will just hold you hostage, and you can tell by the fruits you bare if they are. Are you weary? Tired? Broke? Lonely? Lost? Don't let the ghosts of yesterday haunt you today by not allowing yourself to try something new.

This goes for relationships, lifestyles, health, family and everything in between.

When you look at your current companion, do you still feel butterflies in your belly? Do you get excited every time the phone rings because you want to hear their voice? Of course relationships go through changes, but are you honestly happy? Look at the results of your relationship to determine if whether or not the fruit is blossoming or dying. And let's remember something: just because a person was the perfect companion for you in the past, doesn't necessarily mean they are the perfect companion for you in the present. When you clear away your old identity and begin to build a new version of yourself, your partner might not reflect your current values or be in alignment with what you need to move forward. Thus, when shedding and giving up old ways, we must examine ourselves closely to see what kind of environment we're creating. Is your relationship, career, friendships, and city supporting your current state of growth? If you feel a boost of energy propelling you forward, then continue evolving with what and who you have in your life. But if you're feeling drained, it's a sure sign that certain energies are dragging you down.

Look at the fruits. Are you in distress? Are you always arguing? Do you feel like you're living a lie? Do you say "YES" when you really mean "NO?" And vice versa.

Or... Are you happy? Do you have amazing friends who you trust and confide in? Are you in a loveable relationship? Are you happy in the city and state that you live in? Are you passionate about your career? If the answer is yes and everything is thriving in your life, then you're doing something right. Especially, if you have peace of mind.

Where the holy spirit dwells, there will be increase because God is abundant. Fruits will blossom and your life will become an example for others to follow because you will be inspiring. Furthermore, when you break down the word inspire like "in-spire," it means to be "in spirit." So when you're at peace with yourself and increase flows to you without struggle, that means that your spirit is leading the way which is your "higher self" taking charge. This is true success.

CHAPTER Three: FORGIVENESS

I can tell you from experience that once you forgive someone you've held a grudge with, your vibration instantly increases. It's like a weight lifts off your shoulder and your heart chakra opens up. The spiritual power you gain by loving someone after they've hurt you is not something you can purchase with money or gain credentials with a certificate or diploma. It's something that you do for yourself (sometimes without public recognition) but it will take you very far indeed!

When we talk about discovering and manifesting our life purpose, we can't just be financially wealthy without emotional happiness. To climb the corporate ladder, launch several businesses, purchase comfortable homes and travel the world, you still need to be grounded.

Have you ever heard of rock stars who lost their fame and fortune to drug overdose? AIDS? Suicide? Or bankruptcy? Most of the time, those powerhouse people had some kind of personal dilemma whether it was early childhood trauma, abuse, divorce or some other broken situation that distracted them; whether it was consciously known or subconsciously hidden.

I didn't attract an abusive relationship without first having experienced some type of abuse growing up. Like most modern day families, I come from a divorced one too.

When my parents legally separated, I slept over my grandmother's house most of the time. I've always felt that it was a blessing in disguise because I witnessed firsthand, all of the abuse my grandfather inflicted upon my grandmother.

Why would I consider seeing abuse as a blessing in disguise?

Because it gave me a window into my mother's childhood so that I could understand some of her reactive behavior when she used to lose her temper. (And in understanding her, I began to understand that everyone's behavior stems from their own personal past.) If I could see with my own two eyes, all of the physical and verbal abuse that my grandfather inflicted upon my grandmother, aunts and uncles, then of course, I could only imagine what he had put my mother through when she was growing up – as his first born child.

I watched my grandfather grab a chunk of my aunts hair and drag her across the living room floor just because she wouldn't hang up the phone fast enough with her friend. I saw him break objects in the house and strangle my grandmother's neck until her eyes rolled back, only to have my other Aunt catch an asthma attack to divert the attention away and have everyone go to the hospital. I've seen him throw punches at my uncle, and it made me so angry that I wanted to run away.

Obviously, divorce is no picnic. While both of my parents were rebuilding their new lives separately, I was absorbing everything around me; watching the constant abuse that happened between my grandparents as I stayed with them, and trying to make sense of it all as a preteen.

Eventually, when my mother remarried and got her feet back on the ground, she took me with her when we moved into our new house in Staten Island suburbia. It was a better life, for sure. But by then I had felt the emotional gap within our relationship;

as if we were acquaintance's learning to be relatives again.

As we settled into our new life, I became a typical rebellious teen: I wanted to stay out late, I had a boyfriend she didn't approve of, and I wanted to go to a special Arts High School in Manhattan that she thought was too far away because I'd have to travel outside of the borough. Naturally, I felt powerless during those awkward teen years of trying to develop personal independence while still living underneath someone else's roof.

The older I got, the more I thought she was too strict, and the more she thought I was too rebellious. I hid so many things behind her back that eventually she'd break through my diary and discover secrets about me the hard way.

When my father finally stepped in, he gave me a choice: either stay in Staten Island with my mother, or move to Puerto Rico with his parents for a couple of months to give us some breathing room. Of course, I picked... *la playa!*

During my stay in San Juan, Puerto Rico with my abuelito's on my father's side of the family, I had a lot of time to clear my mind.

My grandfather and I circled the entire island once, driving to every beach we could catch a suntan on from coast to coast, and making pit stops at relatives houses so that I could meet extended family members. Taking in the richness of this tropical island healed my soul in ways that I'll never forget, but it also made me hesitant to return to the states even though I knew I'd have to come back to normality. I hadn't been out of my troubling teenage years yet; I was just on a break.

To be fair, I don't really know too many teens who had it easy with their parents growing up. It's a time when parents either enjoy watching their teens find their own way, or when parents become rattled by losing control over them; especially if the teen doesn't share similar views and interests that the parents would've wanted them to have.

I say all this to say, that eventually as I matured, I forgave my mother. And as connected as me and her are by blood, and as you are to your own parents, everyone has their own special journey – which includes experiences that occurred even before we were born.

FORGIVENESS

It wasn't until I got older that I realized, "How could my mother have all the tools to handle her first born teenage daughter when she had scars that ran so deeply from an abusive father that I saw with my own two eyes, beat up my grandmother?"

At least I knew, without a shadow of a doubt, that she didn't become that way for nothing. She was a survivor. And if being too strict was her way of protecting me from a world she viewed as dangerous because it's what she experienced growing up in an even stricter home, then I had to forgive her. It was her way of loving me the best way she knew how.

If you asked me who I had to forgive, (at that time) it was my mother, but in hindsight, it was my mother's father.

It's so easy to blame our parents for the way our lives turn out. I could say it's her fault for not allowing me to go to a special Arts High School, or her fault for tearing me apart from my High School sweetheart. But I can also look at all the positive ways she made me stronger, like teaching me through example that you should never silence your voice – even though I didn't appreciate how she'd yell at me often; I knew it came from a place of her not being heard when she was a child because her father abused her. In this knowing, I understood that we should never bite our tongue. Time and time again she'd tell me that holding our feelings inside could make us sick and that it was healthier to release them. We might not always like what's coming out, but at least we can see the authenticity of the moment or the person, and then go from there. But if you hold your feelings inside, then you have nothing to work with because people can't read your mind, nor will any real communication take place if you're holding back the truth of what you really feel.

She also taught me not to settle by staying in the old neighborhood forever, and instead, to relocate and upgrade your lifestyle. When she moved to a suburban neighborhood in Staten Island, NY, she proved that removing yourself from the loud noises and hustling energy of the city can help heal your senses; the open space, the nature, and the overall quality of life was safer and healthier, even if it took some time to adjust. In addition, her eating habits changed and she taught me why it was important to be on top of your physical health in both exercise and nutrition. I knew other mothers who ate poorly and suffered from diabetes and other diseases. But my mother became very health conscious; sticking to a routine workout, taking vitamins and supplements, and eating high quality meals because she learned early on in life that no one was going to rescue you.

My mother had a tough childhood, but she created an even brighter future that didn't happen overnight. It took years of surrounding herself amongst positive people and leaving toxic one's behind. She's not afraid to say goodbye to what doesn't serve her, to do what's best for herself, and most of all, she's not afraid to make mistakes while figuring it all out.

Throughout the years, our relationship has healed tremendously; and without having the proper tools to deal with a "troubling teen" because of her own abusive upbringing, she did the best she could with what she knew. Today, as mature women, we've seen the error in our ways and won't go an entire lifetime blaming the other for things gone wrong. We've licked our wounds, forgave each other for being less than perfect, and became better people for it. In fact, because I'm able to love her more deeply after learning about the burning ashes that she's arisen from, I'm able to expand this level of compassion and understanding to the rest of humanity too – because we all have a past, and none of us are exempt from being effected.

If you trace back the origins of abuse, we can travel down the rabbit hole forever – probably since the beginning of time when there were world wars, the great depression, slavery, and so on. Abuse doesn't start with just your parents, or their parents, or even their parents, parents. It literally goes back several generations. For example, I'm sure that my mother's father was abused by his father, and who knows how far back the abuse started? It's not something we're born doing; it's something we're taught.

So who am I going to blame when I've been mistreated? Because the deepest source of where pain comes from is not usually where we think it is. It's so much deeper than what we know. Besides, to pretend that I can't also become that who has hurt me too, would be completely foolish. Hurt people, hurt people. So when looking at who you need to forgive, it is ultimately yourself.

First, forgive yourself for not being perfect enough to graciously love people as unconditionally as let's say, God does. You're human. If you've acted out of character because you retaliated from someone who hurt you, don't beat yourself up. Every cause has an effect. If someone keeps screaming in your face, are you going to be so spiritually immune that it won't affect you one bit? Maybe you screamed back. Maybe you said some things you didn't mean. Maybe you smacked him/her across the face. Maybe you vented and gossiped about it. Maybe you went years without speaking to them. Maybe you blogged about it. Maybe you drank it down. Maybe you cheated and had an affair.

Forgive yourself! If you can't forgive yourself first, how in the world can you forgive others? If you can't show yourself the compassion you deserve for being challenged by situations you weren't prepared for, how can you show others compassion for things they weren't prepared for either?

When you forgive people who hurt you like an abusive parent or an abusive spouse, you free yourself up to attract more positive light into your life; it's like washing your spiritual aura clean.

When you wash your spiritual aura, you'll feel lighter. Thus, success will chase you instead of you chasing it. Don't believe me? Then why do some people walk into amazing situations and when you ask them, "How did that happen?" They reply, "I just happened to be at the right place at the right time!"

It's because they're happy. And when you're all smiles and giggles, other people want to be around you. You get tons of invitations, tons of sponsorships, and tons of gifts because people are drawn to you like a magnet. Hence, with all those opportunities, you're bound to eventually be at the right place at the right time.

But if you carry anger inside of your heart for someone, it effects your aura whether you think it does or doesn't. It doesn't mean that you can't attract good opportunities but there's a ceiling that caps off how high the frequency reaches; but the lighter your spirit and aura is, the higher the frequency will rise in what you'll attract.

Put it this way, think of healthy versus sick. If you've been diagnosed with a disease and your doctor prescribes a set of instructions for you to follow for the next six months that consists of medication, nutrition and exercise, you're going to do it, right? But let's say that after just three months, you decide to stop. That means that even though you may have "improved your health," you're still not completely out of the woods. Thus, if you don't continue following the doctor's instructions completely, you'll slip right back down to where you started. Therefore, you have to be consistent for the entire six months to be completely healthy. Not **half** healthy, but **completely** healthy.

Well, that's how forgiveness works. If you're attracting successful opportunities while holding grudges with people from your past, just imagine how many more opportunities you would attract if you forgave them all? I guarantee that as successful as you already think you are, your success would double and even triple!

Let's also be mindful here: success is not always measured through worldly achievements; meaning, true success doesn't always mean earning a larger salary, a stronger title, expanding your company, gaining more fame or buying another house. (Although it could mean all of those things too). Let's say that your material possessions don't increase, but your health does! Or let's say that your time frees up and you start traveling without having to work, so you suddenly start enjoying life in a way that you never enjoyed it before.

When you forgive others, especially yourself, something inside of you changes – for the better!

Remember, this book is about discovering and manifesting your life "purpose" which drops the ego because we are living in the light. Spiritual light, that is. Thus, the increase that you'll experience will be a true increase within the mind, body and spirit which may or may not reflect material possessions.

You see, there's the illusion that eventually wears off, and then there's the truth that is everlasting.

When your heart opens up to forgive yourself and others, a certain level of wisdom arises that allows you to experience the world in a more colorful way. This means that the things you used to like, you might not even like anymore. Forgiveness makes you warmer, smarter, more approachable, and stronger because it raises your vibration and stretches your consciousness. Just imagine how much better your business relationships would be if people began to receive peaceful vibes from you? Also, imagine how many negative business opportunities you would repel, which would save you from a potential headache?

Would you want to be one of those wealthy professionals spending most of the time in a court room fighting to keep what's yours? Or would you prefer to be a respected professional who doesn't even get mixed up in that type of drama?

Your vibe attracts your tribe.

When you learn to forgive yourself and others, you save yourself a lot of time from having to be a calculative, tough, fake, and aggressive professional who treats business like war. Just think of how much stress it takes to keep up with that? Is it worth all of the material possessions you gain if you lose your soul in the world?

Forgiveness allows you to feel more love. It allows you to be more authentic. It also mends relationships that are meaningful so you don't have to be alone or afraid to trust people again. Yes, people do bad things and I'm not suggesting that you become naïve. But you can be smart, sharp, and respectable without having to lose relationships because you keep people from getting too close.

Remember, forgiveness is only one part of this manual. So it doesn't mean that as soon as you forgive someone that everything will magically become perfect. There are other steps to take that are just as important so that you can discover and manifest your purpose. Also, keep in mind that just because you forgive someone doesn't mean that they have to reciprocate it at the same time. Everyone has their own unique journey which unfolds according to their own freewill that no one has the right to interfere with. Of course, one day, their soul will need to forgive too, but it's not up to anyone to push it upon them. Thus, if you decide to forgive someone who refuses to give up their grudge against you, you shouldn't allow it to affect your aura if your forgiveness for them is REAL.

When you forgive someone, you don't expect them to forgive you back if they won't. You continue with your life and let them know that when they're ready to forgive you, you'll be there. This doesn't mean you stop living your life! No one is a slave. No one is under anyone else's authority. It is your life and you live it the way you want! But if you really and truly forgive someone, then your decision has absolutely nothing to do with their reaction, because you're only responsible for your part.

Easier said than done, right?

FORGIVENESS

I've heard stories from people that have tried to forgive others but the other person continuously made things worse because there was so much hate inside their heart. And no matter how much someone tried to forgive the other person, that person would make it impossible.

Here's the trick. If you really, truly, forgive someone, then you won't look for the type of reaction you want. This has more to do about you then it does about them. However, your forgiveness has to be real. If not, you won't change.

Think of it this way, if you forgive someone but that person still yells, screams, and throws things at you, it shouldn't push you to react the same way because if you mirror back their behavior, then you never really forgave them in the first place. Remember, when you forgive someone, it makes *you more peaceful*. In fact, it makes you inspiring. And others who can't forgive wonder how you're able to do it. They look at you like you have a "super power."

Newsflash! Forgiveness is a "super power" and here's why: A person can ruin your reputation, lie, steal and cheat, but if you forgive them, then their actions will not phase you. And the person who wants to take you down will become more and more annoyed at the fact that nothing they do can hurt you. Can you imagine how strong you must be in order to be unaffected by someone else's malicious attacks?

To love someone beyond their vengefulness means that you're able to look beyond their egoic personality and see the pain they bury deep within, because you understand that only hurt people hurt people. Thus, you feel compassionate towards them and wouldn't want to add to their suffering by fighting fire with fire.

You see, when your cup is overflowing with love, it pours into everyone you meet. But if other people aren't ready to receive it because they're mad, it doesn't mean that you stop overflowing - because you couldn't stop even if you tried. What is natural is natural.

But if you do choose to stop giving love, then you're not overflowing. Because when love overflows, it keeps on giving and giving without needing anything in return.

This doesn't mean that you should beat yourself up if you stopped giving to someone. Acknowledge yourself for being "human" and having limitations. The truth is, that as human beings we do get affected by other people's behaviors which is why conflict exists and why we sometimes retreat. However, after you've acknowledged the fact that your cup may not be overflowing the way it once did, begin the process of replenishing yourself to regain your spiritual power once more. This means that you must forgive yourself and others.

Some helpful tips for forgiving could be:

- Write a letter to the person you're forgiving. You can choose to mail it or not. But when you write down what and why you're forgiving them, it'll help with closure.

- Examine what you learned about yourself from the conflict. How bad is your temper? Do you have little patience? Did you name call? Did you seek revenge? Did you bottle your feelings inside? Did you cheat? What lessons did you learn that will help you understand your own shortcomings?

- Do you think forgiveness is a weak or strong trait? Do you see how it can help you achieve success and why your team or business affiliates will trust you as a person of integrity?

- Do you see how forgiveness brightens up your aura and makes you more attractive by not carrying around stress?

- Before closing the door on someone, try giving them a call to apologize for your part. Whether or not they choose to accept it, at least you can be at peace because you tried.

- Continue living your life without waiting on them to forgive, but the day that they do apologize, do not tell them "It's too late" and continue fighting. That's part of an ego trip. Accept their apology and free them from suffering.

Realize that even the best relationships change, and parting ways is not always a bad thing. For every door that closes, another one opens. But if you're stuck on anger or regret, then you'll never be able to enjoy what the future holds because you haven't set your animosity free. Let the rage go. Let the dead rest. Anger is like dead weight that's a burden to carry on your back. Drop the anger. Whatever it is. It already happened and the past is the past. Let it go and learn to love again. Forgiveness is a huge key in discovering and manifesting your purpose because without it, you'll be blocked and stagnant.

PART 2

Metamorphosis

A change of physical form, structure or substance, especially by supernatural means such as when a caterpillar turns into a butterfly.

CHAPTER *Four:* CLARITY

Singer Johnny Nash sang it best, "I can see clearly now the rain is gone. I can see all obstacles in my way."

Now that you remember your innocence (like a child), you see the fruits of your life (and what you'd like them to look like) and you've learned that the power of forgiveness will brighten up your aura (from the last chapter), you can now gain clarity and create a real vision for your life.

Sometimes we envision the wrong things for ourselves and stay stuck on those goals for years, determined to make it by any means necessary! But if you truly respect your divine purpose for being born, then the things you may want to envision for yourself now might be altered – just a little.

Take me for example:

I wanted to make a hit record, so I wrote a voodoo themed dance song about being possessed on the dancefloor called "Wanting More."

In 2014, the single actually got signed to the reputable label, Nervous Records, and it quickly became a favorite amongst NYC nightclub goers.

Did I manifest that? Absolutely. And even though I could've continued manifesting, something made me question why becoming a famous singer was such a priority in the first place.

I was no longer a 100% focused on becoming an international dance singer like Rhianna or Ariana Grande, even though I knew I could've achieved it had I kept going. Yet something within my subconscious knew that there was a great darkness hidden within the entertainment industry. Jealousy, greed, vanity, drugs, you name it. It was like waving a magic wand within the devil's playground, not realizing that he was the one granting all of my wishes.

Is achieving success positive? Absolutely! There's nothing wrong with fame.

Am I religious? No! But I'm no longer naïve to the wickedness that exists on our planet. So now, when I manifest something, I make sure that it's wholesome and aligned with my spirit's highest good.

Let's say your goal was to become a famous singer, like mine was. If you remember what influenced that dream (from the first chapter of innocence), ask yourself if it is something you still want? And if it is because it came from an intuitive place, then what kind of Singer do you want to be? What image do you want to portray? And what audience do you want to cater to? Sometimes Singers don't care if they're performing for a drug induced crowd where people overdose in front of them. But after I experienced a few mishaps in the industry, I realized how sensitive I am to those environments. Of course it wouldn't be a Recording Artists fault if a person overdosed or drove home drunk from the club. I'm not saying that. But when you're manifesting your dream career, why not make the overall picture as positive as possible?

That's the difference between conscious Artists and unconscious Artists. Are you putting good vibes into the universe? Or are you releasing anything that will sell even if the message doesn't resonate with you?

The same goes for any profession you choose. Whether or not you're a Doctor, Teacher, Lawyer, Entrepreneur, etc., will you be conscious or unconscious? Will you do it solely for the money, the fame and the recognition? Or will you do it for the right reasons? In other words, what are your intentions behind your choices?

Having a "clear vision" for your life means that you feel good about your decisions and that there are no regrets, no doubts, no confusion and no procrastination behind your action. There is no illusion or sacrifice that will hurt you or someone else just to get what you want. If what you desire is wholesome, then it will add value to the world, and the process of making things happen will flow naturally. There might even be a series of coincidences that reveal a path for you to follow as if the universe is approving your choices. The signs will be obvious and you will trust its direction without hesitation.

This is the stage of metamorphosis.

> *When you have gone from unconscious to conscious, you can't be easily manipulated by influences around you. You are growing and leaving behind old ways. This means that you're not just the adult who was once a child, but you are now a being of light who was once living in darkness.*

When people think of living in darkness, right away they think of criminals, rapists, thieves or anything to that extreme. But you don't have to be pure evil to live in darkness. It just means that you may have been ignorant to certain things because you were living to please your ego. You prioritized your fleshly desires over satisfying your spiritual appetite, and there is a big difference between the two.

Becoming a man or woman of the light means that if you knew a higher power was really watching every step you took, he'd be proud of you. It means not being ashamed if people knew the real truth about you. It means that you are authentic and dignified, confident and humble, generous and respected, trusted and admired.

If you made mistakes in the past, this doesn't mean you should carry them forever. That's why the last chapter was about forgiveness because you have to forgive yourself for being human. But once you forgive yourself, then you are able to create a clear vision and begin a new life where you trust your decisions because you are awakened.

People who are unawake (or asleep) make choices based on old programming. They are easily manipulated by society, their parents, social class, pop culture, and the mainstream media. They may seem like they have a fabulous life because that's how it looks on the "outside" but behind closed doors, they suffer from insecurities, abuse, peer pressure, perfectionism, and the need to be accepted. People who lie to themselves are convinced that they got it all together because maybe their bank account is full, they're married, live in a dream house and have all the latest designer shoes and bags, but that doesn't mean that they are truly fulfilled. Something may still be missing. And we've covered this in the earlier chapters.

To have a clear vision is to know who you are, first and foremost. You can't know what you're bringing to the table if you don't really know who you are. So my question is, what has become clear to you? And are you truly clear on who you are and what you want? Because when you're clear, nothing and no one can influence or sway your decisions. To master a clear vision for your life, follow the bullet points below.

- Do you take full responsibility in creating the life you want by trusting your own intuitive voice over outside influences?

- Regardless if you're influenced by mainstream media and your family or your significant other, do you have the courage to change course if you feel propelled to do so? Even if that means changing careers at the height of its success?

- Do you have a clear vision of the kinds of environments you'd like to put yourself in? Do certain invitations now seem unattractive when they once seemed very interesting to attend?

- Do you know what kinds of qualities you look for in a significant other, professional peer and/or friend? Perhaps the types of people you connected with before are not the same kinds of people you connect with now.

- Is there a place you want to visit, whether it's for vacation or to live? Will you give yourself the opportunity to travel to a new environment that may stimulate your senses and open up your horizons? It can be a new country or a different state.

Since our immediate environment has influenced our choices growing up, who's to say that once we step out of our comfort zones, that we won't completely have a change of heart? Or... we might come back and have a new level of appreciation for our home. However, we should at least try to step out of our comfort zone, right?

As you get clear on what you envision for your life, try not to only choose from the things you already know. Try to choose something new so that you can keep growing from new experiences. I always believed that traveling was good for the soul but of course, everyone is different, so don't let me influence you! Hahaha...

But we're talking about "purpose" here; the reason we were brought into this world. How do you know that your purpose will be realized if you stay where you've always been? There's a famous quote that I love.

"Don't stay where you are tolerated. Go where you are celebrated."

But here's the thing. How do you know where you would be celebrated if you don't go somewhere new?

I magnify the word "intuition" a lot because intuitively we all have a feeling that pulls us towards certain places or to do certain things. For example, I might have a pull to visit Europe and join The Arts, but you might have a pull to visit Asia and join animal rights Activism. Hence, intuition is how you'll know what is meant for you, and not for someone else.

Intuition is directly interconnected with purpose. But again, when you unlearn all of your past programming and get clear on your intentions, then your intuition will become stronger and you'll trust its power to reveal your purpose.

As mentioned before, living your life purpose will cause you to add value in the world the same way a flower naturally adds value when it blossoms. And when it blossoms, the flower serves in multiple ways such as the following: healing diseases with medicinal benefits, being a token of romance when given as a gift, perfuming the air with its aroma, and being a symbol of sympathy at funerals. In that same regard, each living person has a purpose for why they were born. There is something that their presence gives, something that they do, say, or create that adds to the evolution of this world.

Intuitively, you'll feel a sense of knowing what you were put on earth for. And when you do, you must stay "clear" by not allowing yourself to become distracted by temptation.

What kind of temptation? The kind that will bring you back to old programming which is based on fear, acceptance, and ego based living. Thus, when you live from the ego based platform, your intuition will quiet down until you won't be able to hear it anymore because you'll be inside of your head. And in order to hear your intuition, it will come from your spirit and heart center, not your head. This doesn't mean to dismiss all logic. What it does mean however, is that first you follow your intuition, secondly you open up your heart, and thirdly you make reason with all of it. Your spirit should always lead first and foremost, not the other way around. And yes, your heart is always at the center, in the middle, and never last!

Now that you should be clear on what you want because your desires are healthy and wholesome, and you have the courage to make major life changes if necessary, now

Living In The Light

you can do the most courageous thing ever – take a leap of faith!

CHAPTER

Five:

LEAP OF FAITH

❝When the student is ready, the teacher will appear," is one of my favorite Buddhist quotes. The reason is quite simple; because everything that happens to us happens at the perfect moment in time; not a minute before or after.

When you take a leap of faith, you jump into the unknown, vulnerable and naked like a newborn baby. It is there, in your courage, when the universe will support you by bringing you a teacher.

No one can make it on their own. We all need help. Despite the fact that we must make decisions by ourselves, we are not left to live our entire existence alone, obviously. But as we interact with many people throughout our lives, there are those few in between who are called "teachers" that just happen to show up at the right place at the right time when we need them the most.

Have you ever wanted to do something brand new but stopped yourself out of fear of what could go wrong?

It was my supervisor who encouraged me to travel alone. When I was deciding on how to use my vacation days from work, he told me not to wait for others and that I would enjoy going away - even if by myself. That's when I bought a coach bus ticket to stay at Ananda Ashram - the Yoga Retreat upstate NY.

I enjoyed myself so much that when I returned, I decided to take it a step further by purchasing a plane ticket to Sedona, Arizona. My family was a little nervous about me traveling across country, but the momentum was already taking over.

The experience I had, driving down a twirling road amidst red rock mountains underneath a purple majestic sky, was nothing short of divine. It was a huge change from the NYC brownstone life; open road, green cactus plants, warm weather to detoxify my body, and fresh, clean breathing air.

I'll never forget the peace that filled my heart so much, that I could've cried from joy. The world seemed perfect; like the heaven I knew it could be.

Although I could've joined a group tour guide, I decided to bravely hike up one of the mountains alone: Bell Rock. With a backpack, strapped up hiking boots, and a rolling tripod for filming, I hiked the trail only to be met with a dust storm that appeared out of nowhere. My heart dropped as the wind fiercely twirled faster and faster, blowing insane amounts of dust into my face. I quickly got out of the area and met a woman who was coincidently driving to my next destination: The Holy Chapel. It's a famous church that is built within the mountains overlooking the town of Sedona. She asked me if I wanted a ride, and of course, I accepted.

While sitting on the mountain top, in front of the entrance to this spiritual sanctuary, I had a conversation with my creator; just me and him, alone.

I thanked him for my life, for my health, for my finances, for my peace of mind, and for the opportunity to allow me to experience such a gorgeous town. That's when I asked him for another favor; if I could take my spiritual journey a bit deeper by visiting the actual holy land of Israel.

I'd have to face a major fear for that one because I wouldn't just be traveling across the country, but I'd be *leaving* the country.

Funny how life works, but not even one month later, as I was back home lying in bed inside of my Brooklyn apartment, I went on a dating app and met an Israeli man who shocked the hell out of me from our very first encounter.

As God is my witness, his ethnicity wasn't even mentioned on his profile, nor did I guess it through photos alone. He just looked like a handsome, caramel skinned man who lived not too far from me.

Even though we lived close, we spoke on the phone for hours before meeting in person. I don't think it was intended to be that way; but we were so curious about each other that we couldn't stop talking once we started.

As any first conversation goes, we asked the usual questions about where we're from and what we do for a living, and once he told me that he was born in Israel, I instantly lit up! My voice peeked up a level as I expressed my deep desire to visit his native land, and he was so impressed, that he decided to teach me Hebrew every day.

I didn't believe him at first, nor did I believe that I could learn how to speak (what seemed to be) such a complicated language, but he insisted that it was actually easier than I thought.

My passion to learn made me jump at the opportunity, and every night before he went to sleep, he'd text me a new Hebrew sentence along with the English translation to which I'd reply, "Toda Raba," which means "Thank you so much," and "Lyla Tov," which means "Goodnight."

In the mornings, we'd repeat with "Boker Tov," and he'd sprinkle new words every day until we were speaking Hebrew without me needing to pause, think, or ask him what it meant... Ok, so I wasn't in Israel yet, but I felt that the universe had brought him to me in order to prepare my journey ahead. I mean, what are the chances that I'd meet an Israeli man just one month after I prayed to God on an Arizona mountain top about visiting the holy land?

As I currently write this book, the world is under the COVID19 pandemic. Thus, my plans to Israel won't happen immediately but that doesn't mean that it won't happen in the future. However, meeting that man who took the time out to teach me his language in such a quick matter of time was proof of how the universe not only answers our prayers, but how it sends us helpers, so that we're never alone.

For example, there are people who packed their bags and left everything behind, driving across country to move to an entirely new state where they knew absolutely no one, all because they followed their intuitive hunch. Despite the fear, they moved anyway and happened to meet a special person along the way who helped them do what they couldn't have done alone.

These are teachers, angels and guides. Whenever you decide to take a leap of faith in any area of your life that is foreign to you, the universe will not leave you alone in darkness. For the very act of you taking action from trusting your own intuition is enough to bring you into alignment with more love and light that will come in the form of support.

Some examples are of the following:

- A man or woman finds the courage to leave their long term ten-year marriage, but meets someone incredible immediately after the divorce (and sometimes while still legally separated.)

- A person quits a very secure corporate job without any backup, and is suddenly offered another opportunity that flowed naturally to him/her.

- A person leaves a prestigious University with a promising future, but ends up becoming a prominent public figure (like Alicia Keys who passed up an education at Columbia University but became a successful Grammy Award winning Recording Artist.)

Some people might think these things happen to one out of a million people but I beg to differ. The truth is that it's about following your intuition which I can't stress enough. We can't just walk out of situations if we don't feel right about it like irresponsible and dramatic people. But when you feel "intuitively compelled" with a deep pull to do something drastic, that's when you shouldn't doubt your gut!

Hence, when you take this leap of faith to follow your gut, there is always someone there that just happens to show up – at exactly the perfect time!

However, I'm not suggesting that you should be waiting anxiously for this person to arrive because, it's never about someone else. It's always about you. And even when that person does show up when you need them, get ready to go up another level by learning some lessons that you didn't expect to learn – and it might not always be as easy to adapt to as you think.

SIDE NOTE: some lessons are so hard that they need to be relearned twice.

Fear not; big problems are small to a giant. And this is why when you gather up the courage to take a leap of faith, you are sending signals to the universe that you're ready to grow, or else you would've remained in your comfort zone. Therefore, whatever teacher comes to you, no matter how tough the lesson may be, they are there as a gift to motivate, expand, and stretch you into someone who will eventually become a giant.

And what giant became a giant by remaining too afraid to take a leap of faith? So you see, there is nothing to fear.

Now... let's say that as you're manifesting your purpose, you've realized that it's to become an Actress but you're too afraid to ditch your stable job of security, too afraid of moving out of state to audition (in let's say Los Angeles), too afraid to invest into acting classes, and too afraid to leave a relationship that probably prevents you from exploring that side of yourself.

If you've read the beginning of this book then you should have confidence in being clear about what you want, you should be able to forgive those who don't see your vision by not taking their lack of support personally, and you should have the courage to make the changes you need to have for a fruitful life – that is – to have a life that multiples instead of decreases.

Sometimes we have to leave our old environments that stagnate us in order to thrive in a new environment that will set our hearts on fire – with a plan.

So, let's take pursuing a career in film for example. There are plenty of jobs that offer flexible hours. Whether this means becoming a bartender or a waitress which is extremely common amongst actors, there's a reason why they take those shifts and you can't be afraid to make a little sacrifice to gain something bigger. But if you're afraid that you can fall under the trap of never getting your "big break", then create your own opportunities such as, earning your College degree in film so if you ever hit a financially low point with acting, you can still earn money teaching it while still maintaining a flexible schedule for auditioning. Teaching rather than bartending in order to make ends meet, keeps you within the energy sphere of your chosen field.

That was just an example of pursuing a career in film. But with anything in life, it's all about breaking old habits to create new "healthy" habits that will align you with who you are, what you want, and what you're great at!

Another example of taking a leap of faith is confessing the truth after a lie. It could be that you've been spending rent money on abusing drugs or alcohol and you need help to recover from this addiction. Your confession might hurt someone you love if you've been hiding it from them, but the truth will set you free.

It could also be that you've been having an affair on your wife or husband. Although you might lose them, you might also keep them because confessing this truth might actually make your marriage stronger than it was before. What's the point in coming home to a miserable life when you can either end it, or make the real improvements necessary that will prevent you from seeking love elsewhere?

There are a number of scenarios of how telling the truth will set you free, but it takes a leap of faith to let go of your skeletons in the closet. When you do, you'll realize how spiritually strong you are for not being deceitful. Hence, we attract what we are. So when you're honest with others, you give them permission to be honest with you – or you attract a new set of honest people while your old crowd falls away because they no longer match your frequency.

Before taking a leap of faith, ask yourself these 3 things:

- Does your intuition encourage this decision? In other words, does it just feel right even when everyone else says it's wrong?

- If for some reason, things didn't work out as you had thought, would you still be glad you took the chance?

- Are you being honest with the people who may be involved with your decision to act on this leap of faith, or are you hiding something just so you can have your way?

- If there is something you need to confess, are you trusting your intuition to say things at the right time? Confessing something that may hurt someone still needs to be handled with sensitivity. But blurting it out at the wrong time just to get it off your chest, doesn't help make it better.

Taking a leap of faith into the unknown requires an honest heart to be able to navigate through the darkness. It's like going to a new country where you don't know the language, the customs, or the laws. One of the ways you can keep yourself safe is by recognizing when someone's intentions are off. But how would you know if someone's intentions are off, if yours are off too? The more real, brave, and clear you are, the sharper your instincts will be because you'll recognize when others are being sincere, and when they're not.

Unfortunately, some people will pretend to have your best interest at heart because they notice that you're being vulnerable by taking a leap of faith. A manipulative person will use your honesty against you. This is where your light must shine brighter than the darkness that's trying to lower your frequency. Will you get tricked? Will you be fooled? Will you trust the wrong person who offers you a helping hand when you're out there on new territory? In fact, what if you're one of those people who left your spouse for another (in a leap of faith) but then realized that it was a mistake? Taking a leap of faith doesn't always mean that things happen exactly how we pictured it in our minds.

This bring us to our next chapter: LOVE.

CHAPTER Six: LOVE

Is love total freedom? Or is love possession? I think love is a choice, which makes it a little bit of both – almost.

In Bram Stokers "Dracula" (1992), there's a scene where the main character Mina openly confesses to Dracula that she's willing to enter the dark side to see what he sees, feel what he feels, know what he knows and be who he is. Although it's what Dracula always wanted to hear, he struggles for a moment by resisting her.

Dracula never pushes a victim away! So why did he consider rejecting this one? In this unforgettable performance of inner transformation, his response to her was, "No, I must not... I cannot... allow you to join me. I love you *too much.*"

We see here, that he did something he would never normally do because something *inside* of him changed. Isn't that would love does? Change us?

Perhaps then, love is a miracle.

Love is the hand that reaches out to help the unloved. It gives someone a reason to rethink suicide. It reverses sickness because of laughter and support. It's a miracle, indeed. Because at the highest levels of watching love-in-action, you become moved by something greater than yourself.

It takes a strong will-power and conscious intellect to understand why love is always the best choice in any situation. It has the power to transform lives and even influence the world as it's done for many years. But love is not for the weak or cowardly. It's actually for the fearless.

Knowing that you can die when protecting someone you love from being harmed, is an act of sacrifice which brings you into another dimension. Not only through physical death (in the literal sense) but also through spiritual death when leaving behind an old "comfortable" way of being to become "uncomfortable" for something bigger than yourself. In the example of Dracula, we see how Mina chose to leave behind her world of safety and comfort in order to join Dracula and understand life through his eyes. But because he knew the evilness of whence he came, he rejected her offer in order to protect her innocence.

This leads me to the topic of lost souls, abusers, and the possessed.

Even those certain toxic personalities we've come to label as the following:

- overt narcissists
- covert narcissists
- psychopaths
- sociopaths and abusers of any kind

They too are human beings who have lost their way and would need the mercy of a supernatural power to cast away their demons. But to deem anyone as unforgiveable, blocks the stream of a powerful love.

Now, I don't suggest accepting abuse and maintaining a relationship with a toxic person! Please do not misunderstand or misinterpret this message.

People who behave at low frequencies should be handled with discernment. In fact the truth is, these troubled souls are our greatest teachers in disguise because they test our buttons. Do you *understand* why they're short tempered and where their reactions stem from? Or do you think they're just crazy without reason? Do you *speak up* for yourself when they've put you down or do you stay quiet out of fear? Do you *confidently walk away* when they've disrespected you or do you walk on egg shells and stay as long as they demand? Do you disregard *your own intuition* and *sense of reasoning* because they want you to believe their side of the story every time they argue with other people?

A person who sacrifices out of fear and obligation is not choosing their actions out of love, and therefore there won't be any transformation or miracle. In fact, it will do the opposite. It will decrease your energetic aura and continue to enable the person who is causing the drama.

We can learn a lot about ourselves when being challenged by an abuser because of how we deal with certain situations. It tests our strength, our intelligence, our will-power, our grace, our courage, and our own understanding of the entire human species as a collective.

Let's focus on a Narcissist for a moment. Although there are two main types:

1. The ones who grew up extremely smothered and spoiled, being the "favorite", always getting their way and

being the center of attention in everything, to then feel superior when they reach adulthood and look down on others because they believe their better and deserve more than the rest.

OR

2. The ones who suffered traumatic childhoods so severe and neglectful that they had to aggressively take in order to survive which shaped them into cold hearted individuals who view love as a weakness. Because of this, they seek to control others with manipulative tactics in order to protect their fragile ego from experiencing another heartache, loss or other type of abandonment.

When you understand the background of a Narcissist and how they came to be, it should inspire some compassion in the knowing that they're not just bad people without a soul. They're human beings who have learned a specific behavioral pattern that has now become a personality or mental disorder. What does this have to do with you? Well... If you're someone who does not have a personality or mental disorder, then you wouldn't look down on people who do.

Let's circle this back to love.

I mentioned before that love is a miracle. It's something that is of a higher dimension which causes healing and transformation as if by magic, and perhaps it is. Love is activated by a belief, a force so strong that the energy behind it transcends a negative into a positive.

If you look at Science, it's always the dominant energy that pushes out the lesser one. This means, that if negativity is the dominant force, then positivity will leave or be crushed. But, if positivity is the dominant force, then the negativity will leave or be crushed.

So when dealing with the Dracula's of the world, the difficult people, the untrustworthy and the broken, do we allow the energy of fear to chase us away? Or do we get as much help as possible from other loving souls that – through the power of unconditional love – can overwhelm someone with good energy from a collective unit?

I don't suggest that you love a dark criminal all by yourself if you've already seen the damage they can do. Be realistic. That's a trap for abuse. But if a group of people all wrapped their arms around a criminal and showed mercy upon him, then perhaps this kind of proof that love does exist would give the "criminal" or "bad person" motivation to turn over a new leaf.

It's about the dominant energy.

It's about multiplying.

It's about increase.

So which wolf will you feed, because the one you starve will die but the one you feed will thrive. Feed love. And oh! This doesn't mean that love is weak which is exactly where people get it twisted.

Love is tough. Love is justice. Love is smart. Love is clear. Love is grounded. Love is transformational. Love is creative. Love is all inclusive. Love is brave. Love is medicine. Love is life. Love is a miracle.

Here's the trick. There are of course, certain people that no matter how much love you surround them with, they will still be determined to kill a good thing. Yes, unfortunately, some people are just so damaged that no matter what anyone else does, it is ultimately their choice to self-destruct. In this case, you have to love a person enough to let them go or put them away in order to protect others. But when you do this, it's done with compassion and that's the difference between "tough love" and "being just as bad as them."

What about healthy relationships that aren't so extreme? The normal, balanced and stable relationships? Does it mean that there's real love since they're nontoxic? Not necessarily. Just because something looks good doesn't mean it is.

You, yourself, must know what love is in order to recognize when it's false. Love is a ride that will take you on a journey into the unknown. But they'll be a feeling within that tells you, you can trust it; that it's right for you. But if you're not being inspired, if you're not growing in some way, if you're becoming bored or stagnant in your life, then real love isn't there. It's the reason why so many couples get divorced, or people move far away, or suddenly switch careers. It's because they realize that somethings missing. When you look at a life line, it squiggles up and down to let you know that there's a heartbeat. But once it becomes a "flat line", it means death.

Love gives you a heartbeat.

It gives you air. It gives you inspiration. It gives you purpose.

In fact, I believe that sometimes we don't choose love. Love chooses us.

People cross our paths who we never saw coming. Will you be the one to join their world? Or will they be the one to join yours? In a universe where everything is connected, all it takes is one person to open your eyes to a different perspective. Without them, you may have never thought of things that way before or been exposed to such a way. Love will change you, that's for sure. It won't leave you the same way it found you.

Before telling someone you love them, ask yourself these things:

- Do you expect them to love you back? Or are you completely fine whether or not they do?
- Are you prepared to go through storms together? To be their rock as a friend, lover or spouse?
- Have you lost yourself within them or are you stronger than you've ever been before because of them?
- If you confess that you love them, will it make things better or worse

if other people are involved and the timing is off?

- Does your experience with them make you feel like a better person? And do you know if their experience with you makes them feel like a better person?

Love will always be about increase. Increase in expanding your perspectives, increase in opening up your heart, increase in becoming inspired, increase in trying a new way, and increase in feeling more vitality.

This may sound crazy to some, but I have two cats for pets who have increased my life tremendously by allowing me the opportunity to give them the best life as a pet parent. When I searched for a new apartment, I needed one that allowed pets or I wasn't moving in. When I dated people, I looked for men who weren't allergic and if they were, they'd take allergy pills because I'd never give my cats away. That's a deal breaker. In a sense, my pets have taught me about what we're willing to sacrifice for love because I'm responsible for them. You wouldn't give your children away if a man didn't want to date a woman with kids, would you?

Sure, pets are not human. But there are those who see the value that pets add to the family while others don't. Love will open your mind and change your perspective on things. What's wrong with loving animals as much as you love humans? Just because they're different doesn't mean they don't deserve to be prioritized. I have an unspeakable bond with my pets that go beyond the limits of vocal language. I can feel what they need when they rub against my leg and purr for some food. I can tell when they don't like a specific visitor by the way they try to grab my attention by scratching the door, trying to communicate that they want the person to leave. I know when they want me to feel better by sleeping on top of my chest after watching me cough and sneeze from a bad cold. I don't direct them to me; they come on their own when they see me sick.

Love is a frequency we tune into and it's all around us. What do you love? What and who has given your life increase? And in what ways have you increased someone else's? That's amore!

CHAPTER

Seven:

PASSING THE TORCH

We started the first chapter of this book with the cycle of life and death by describing my new found possibility of conceiving a child after, coincidently, my ex fiancé passed away. There's no better way to show how the universe connects these two polar opposites by allowing one door to close while another opens, creating space for a new soul to enter earth through the womb.

And as these new souls enter earth with a fresh, clean slate, what will they learn... from us?

You don't keep information to yourself; you pass it on. Like creatures who multiply because it's the law of nature, we give birth to continue life. Movement continues. Energy continues. Life continues.

Remember how the first chapter spoke of children being taught certain things because their parents pass down their own beliefs and opinions of what their child should grow up to become? And that even with the best of intentions, sometimes adults give the wrong guidance? It's no one's fault, really, because parents were once children too and they're just passing down what was passed down to them. The question is, what will you pass down?

Will you teach your children, neighbors, students, employees, and audiences that there's a difference between things that are wholesome and things that are toxic? Will you express the fact that even though there's much cruelty in the world, it doesn't mean you need to blend in and become the same in order to make it? Will you pass down certain cultural beliefs even if you know their harmful to the mind, or will you let certain things die off in order to create a new world?

When the spirit is nourished and charged with positive energy, it can't help but to inspire wherever it goes because it's natural. It's like the Sun lighting up the world or a flower exuding its fragrance. There's no way it couldn't! The very nature of something is going to fulfill its purpose because it's not designed to do anything else. So when you are living in alignment with your highest self - and by this I mean - your most peaceful self, you are going to inspire others by being a living example of that spark.

The thing is this, people are impressionable. They get inspired by anything they think will heighten their value, and that includes teenagers trying to fit in with the "cool" kids at school. That can involve doing drugs, smoking cigarettes, being initiated into a gang, and doing all sorts of toxic things. Being easily influenced doesn't stop as an adult because people will exploit others just to get to the top; we see it in governmental politics all the time. Inspired to become President of The United States, people will crush their opponent's spirit and it's expected of both candidates to behave the same in order to win! So when passing the torch of inspiration, will you pass the torch of inner peace or false pride?

No one said that taking the higher road would be easy. But the more people do the "right thing," the less the "wrong thing" would be acceptable and considered normal. And why do we wait for someone else to be the brave soul or pioneer to create the change we seek? Why can't we just get ourselves into alignment, soul search, and reinvent ourselves if need be? Even if it takes a while and makes us uncomfortable at first, it's so worth it in the end. This is the best way to pass the torch. It's by being a living example.

When you're amongst friends, family and professional social circles, do you entertain conversations about celebrity gossip and people bashing? Or are you the one to gently change the subject without making anyone feel bad by diverting their attention to a more positive subject? When you hear people making racial remarks, do you also joke with them about that specific ethnic group, or do you throw in a statement to show how the shoe can easily be on the other foot because we're all the same? What kind of energy will you bring into situations? Will you raise the vibe, give hope, inspire change, give light to ignorance?

When discovering and manifesting your life purpose, passing the torch is inevitable. But of course, there are those you will inspire more greatly than others. It may be your children, your students, your fans, or even your spouse. Anyone whom you have a closer relationship with will receive more of your insight. When you have this much influence, (intertwined in someone else's life) you must understand that there's a responsibility that comes with it. The words you choose to say in the tone you decide to vocalize it has the power to make someone feel better or worse, and to make them adopt your beliefs and spread them throughout the world.

Picture yourself as a mentor even if you think you're not. There's always someone watching you, even if you don't know who. Until something horrible happens (and I hope it doesn't) people sometimes don't realize why it's so important to live righteously with integrity and honor. It's only until they hit rock bottom or something seriously unlucky happens that they then realize, life is not all glamour and glitz. So yes, play your part in bringing some truth and substance back into conversations that will open our eyes to the bigger picture of life. If you really want to discover and manifest your life purpose, know that you're here to serve just like the Sun that lights the earth, rising each day for a brand new beginning.

When passing your torch of knowledge, gifts, experiences and wisdom, ask yourself...

- Is this the right thing to teach even though it may be the harder thing to do? Or is it the wrong thing to teach even though it's easier to do because it's normalized?

- Is what you're passing down going to be of use in the long term after you've passed away? Or will it only be of use during a certain phase like a fashion accessory that will be "in today" and "out tomorrow?"

- Is what you're teaching going to enhance someone else's life or only enhance yours?

Empty out your vessel if need be and allow the light of source energy to flow through you so that you're filled up with the goodness and power of a higher love. If something bigger is pouring down blessings upon you, then wouldn't you want to also pour down blessings upon others?

When I was going through a tough break up, a friend of mine introduced me to a Reiki Master. I had always been curious as to how Reiki works since it doesn't involve touching the body, so I figured that I had nothing to lose since I was already experiencing a heartbreak. Little did I know, Reiki heals as naturally as the sun lights the sky.

Reiki is an "energy healing" technique that is transferred through the palms of the hand when placed slightly above certain areas of the body. It is said that the universal life force energy flows through the hands to activate self-healing within the patient. And to be honest, it's true!

Now, whether you believe in the practice of Reiki or not is not the main point; it is about the practice of passing something down to others in order to heal, uplift, and raise the vibrations.

I had been crying over yet another ex whom I thought would've stuck around for the long haul. I've had my share of traumatic experiences as I described earlier in the book, but this man was someone I considered a friend; someone whom I thought that even if it didn't work out romantically, we could've still left off on a positive note being able to maintain a platonic friendship. For some reason, the pain of us parting ways reminded me of my other ex who had died. Maybe something triggered my memory, but whatever it was, I wasn't ready to let go in the manner that we did. It felt as if our misunderstanding had gotten blown out of proportion and like our ending wasn't fair.

The Reiki Master who treated me did it through a zoom face meeting online. First, she instructed me to smudge some sage, light a candle, and lay down on a yoga mat in an area where I would be undisturbed for at least an hour. Placing my cell phone on the ground beside my body, I rested on top of my yoga mat with eyes closed, and followed her voice as she spoke.

Laying down in the middle of my living room floor eased my stress. Sometimes we don't realize how much our body needs a break; even our mind from all of the mental chatter.

When ready, the Reiki Master then played a song of a woman chanting to let go of everything that no longer serves you. Her words of letting go echoed through my mind like a hypnotism as it played repeatedly for the first 30 minutes, putting my spirit in a state of ease, ensuring that all was as it should be.

I suddenly realized that there was no reason for me to hold on so tightly to something that was swept away from me so naturally. It's like the wind that blows the hat off your head; there are things we have no control over, and when it's time to leave, they just do. Why run after them or agonize over what's gone?

The universal life force energy is always moving forward because it constantly expands, stretches and grows. This is life. This is vitality. This is energy. This is Reiki.

What is dead stops growing. In fact, it shrivels up and shrinks until disappearing completely, sometimes returning to the earth to then recycle itself and begin again. But when it does begin again, it grows again.

When the Reiki Master went into the deeper part of the treatment, she told me not to open my eyes for the remainder of the session. As God is my witness, I felt a swirl of energy circling my feet until this energetic ring began to travel upwards throughout my entire body. It was warm and tingly, and felt unreal. In fact, it felt so unreal, that after the treatment was done, I no longer felt sadness or regret for the breakup. It was like something within me had awoken, like a candle suddenly being lit with a match.

The Reiki Master told me that all she did was activate what was already within me. It wasn't that she transferred her own energy into me; it was that she had healed my own.

This is what it means to pass the torch. We don't have to lose a piece of ourselves or burn ourselves alive trying to keep someone else warm. We simply pass on the gifts we've been given to others so that they can realize their own potential and their own purpose.

None of us are meant to inhabit this planet forever; it's not our forever home. At the beginning of this book, I made reference to the biblical scripture, "Although we live in the world, we are not of the world," (2 Corinthians). Hence, our physical death is not the death of our spirit; it is just a transition into another place for our journey to continue. So while we're here, making our way through this thing called "life," why not pass the torch of universal love and truth?

When you are burning bright like the North Star, pass that torch and blaze a trail into the right direction. The ones who know where to look will find the magic and live in greatness.

BIO

Beginning her career as an independent Recording Dance Artist with several singles sold worldwide, Jasmine Clemente, has metamorphosis into a creative business woman owning hometomysoul, LLC. She lives in Brooklyn, NY handcrafting floral scented candles that represent the light within humanity. A Lightworker, Reiki Practitioner, Yoga Teacher, Motivational YouTuber and Sultry Singer, she inspires to make a difference through various creative outlets and enlightened works. Visit www.hometomysoul.com to get some of those juicy vibes! She also makes handmade sage bundles and other holistic goodness. Her instagram is @jasmineclemente and @hometomysoul

Living In The Light

www.ingramcontent.com/pod-product-compliance
Lightning Source LLC
Chambersburg PA
CBHW022114090426
42743CB00008B/840